JESSE OWENS

TOM STREISSGUTH

**In Consultation with Martha Cosgrove,
M.A. and Reading Specialist**

LERNER PUBLICATIONS COMPANY / MINNEAPOLIS

Martha Cosgrove has a master's degree from the University of Minnesota in secondary education, with an emphasis on developmental and remedial reading. She is licensed in 7–12 English and language arts, developmental reading, and remedial reading. She has had several works published, and she gives numerous state and national presentations in her areas of expertise.

Lerner Publications Company
A division of Lerner Publishing Group
241 First Avenue North
Minneapolis, Minnesota U.S.A.

Website address: www.lernerbooks.com

Library of Congress Cataloging-in-Publication Data

Streissguth, Thomas, 1958–
  Jesse Owens / by Tom Streissguth.
    p.   cm. – (Just the facts biographies)
  Includes bibliographical references and index.
  ISBN: 0-8225-2256-X (lib. bdg. : alk. paper)
    1. Owens, Jesse, 1913–Juvenile literature. 2. Track and field athletes–United States–Biography–Juvenile literature. I. Title. II. Series.
  GV697.O9S87 2005
  796.42'092–dc22   2004002618

Manufactured in the United States of America
1 2 3 4 5 6 – JR – 10 09 08 07 06 05

Contents

1

WATCHED
BY THE WORLD

(Above)
Jesse
Owens at the
1936
Olympic
Games in
Berlin

IN EARLY AUGUST 1936, Jesse Owens won his first Olympic gold medal by running the 100-meter dash in 10.3 seconds. He was at the Summer Olympic Games in Berlin, the capital of Germany. In the next few days, Owens won three more golds–in the 200-meter dash, in the broad jump, and in the 400-meter relay. He was the first track athlete ever to win four gold medals at a single session of the Olympic Games.

Owens won fame and respect for these Olympic feats. But in 1936, his victories meant more than who could run the fastest. Owens ran his races in front of Adolf Hitler, the leader of Germany. Hitler and his Nazi Party believed that Germans were superior to all other people. He especially thought German white athletes were better than African Americans like Jesse Owens.

The 1936 Olympic Games in Berlin were supposed to show off Nazi ideas and power. The Games were also designed to tell the world how well Germany had come back from its defeat in World War I (1914–1918). German soldiers marched at the start of the Games. The soldiers symbolized the country's military power. Hitler expected German athletes to win and to show the world the strength of the German people.

The Nazi Party used swastikas (on the banners at right) to stand for Nazi ideas and power.

In the days before the Games started, reporters and fans arrived from all over the world. They had come to watch the "Nazi Olympics." Many of these people liked how clean the country was and how well things were run. The world was struggling through the Great Depression, a time of serious economic hardship. Many people greatly admired Germany's ability to stage and pay for the Olympic Games. These people wondered if any other country could have done it. Maybe the Nazis' belief in their own superiority could be true after all.

Then, on that day in August, Jesse Owens took his starting position. The world was watching. And Jesse Owens's life would change forever.

EARLY DAYS

Jesse Owens came from Oakville, a town in north-central Alabama. In the early 1900s, Oakville was a farming community in the South. About one hundred white and black families worked hard to grow crops on small plots of land. Many of the farmers were sharecroppers. They didn't own their land. Instead, they gave the cotton and corn they raised to the landowner to pay their rent. Most

Life as a sharecropper wasn't much different from slavery. In this picture, a man, instead of a horse, pulls a plow.

Oakville farmers struggled to keep food on their tables and roofs over their heads.

Jesse was born James Cleveland Owens on September 12, 1913. He was the last of ten children (three daughters and seven sons) born to Henry and Emma Owens. His family called him J.C. J.C.'s first home was a small wooden house. Soon after his birth, the family moved to a larger farm. They

An exact copy of Jesse's Alabama house sits in a park created in his honor.

still were sharecroppers, using their crops to pay the rent to a landowner.

The Owens's new house was hot in summer and cold in winter. The floors were bare wooden planks. The children usually walked barefoot, so J.C. was often sick with colds and other lung problems. He also had painful boils on his skin.

IT'S A FACT!

J.C. often had pneumonia when he was young. This disease weakens the lungs. Later on, when J.C. was training in track, he had to work especially hard to strengthen his lungs.

The Owenses didn't have the money to pay for a doctor's visit. J.C.'s mother would cut open the boils with a hot kitchen knife. This action was thought to speed up the healing of the skin.

Even though his family was poor, J.C. had a happy boyhood. He was free to run in the fields and forests near his house. "I always loved running," he remembered. "I wasn't very good at it, but I loved it because it was something you could do all by yourself, and under your own power. You could go in any direction, fast or slow as you wanted, fighting the wind if you felt like it, seeking out new sights just on the strength of your feet and the courage of your lungs."

Young J.C. wasn't as happy about school. He had trouble learning to read, and he often skipped school. Each year, when the planting and harvesting seasons came around, schools closed. Jesse and other students worked in the fields. The seasonal shutdown cut back on how many days he spent at school. As a result, he didn't learn as much.

MOVING TO CLEVELAND

The Owenses worked hard on their farm. But every year, they had to give half their crops to the landowner to pay the rent. They had less food to eat or to sell. They didn't have enough money to buy their own land. They were always in debt. Any extra money was for buying clothing and other necessary things. J.C.'s clothing was old and had been mended many times. His ragged shirts and pants embarrassed him.

J.C.'s mother believed the family could find a better life somewhere else. She wanted to move away from Oakville someday. She wanted to give her children a chance at a good education and decent jobs.

Mrs. Owens had heard about the busy factories and large businesses in cities such as Detroit, Michigan, and Chicago, Illinois. These cities were far from Alabama and far from the Owenses' friends and family. But one of the Owenses' children, a daughter named Lillie, had moved north to Cleveland, Ohio. Lillie's letters home convinced her mother that the rest of the family should move there too. In the early 1920s, the Owens family packed up and headed north by train.

When they arrived in Cleveland, the Owenses moved into a small apartment on the East Side. Black families and immigrants from Poland, Italy, and other

Cleveland, like many other large cities, drew sharecroppers away from their farms. The farmers hoped to find a better life.

distant countries lived in the neighborhood. The Owenses found jobs, but their wages were low. Like everyone else on the East Side, they had to work hard to pay their bills.

Emma Owens and some of her daughters worked as maids. "My brothers found odd jobs on the same level," J.C. remembered, "from unloading freight cars to [working as] part-time janitors. One by one, they had to drop out of school to help bring enough money in for all of us." J.C. was able to stay in school. But he took

many different part-time jobs. He worked in a
shoe shop and delivered groceries. He took care
of plants in a greenhouse.

J.C. had already gone to school in Oakville. But
when he got to Cleveland, he had to start all over.
Even though he was nine, he was placed in first
grade at Bolton Elementary School. The school's
principal and teachers were sure that he would have
to work hard to catch up with other students his age.
But in a short time, J.C. moved up to the second
grade. One of his teachers couldn't understand his
strong Alabama accent. This teacher turned "J.C."
into Jesse.

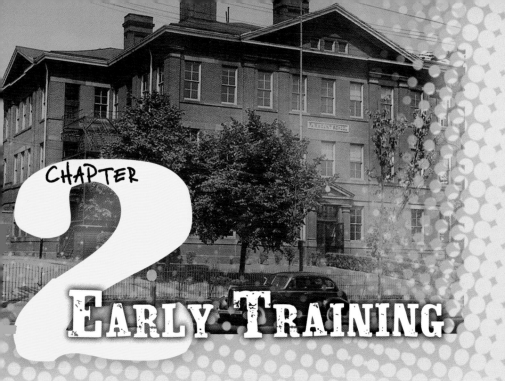

CHAPTER 2
EARLY TRAINING

AFTER BOLTON ELEMENTARY, Jesse went to Fairmount Junior High. He didn't read well, but he advanced with the other students in his class. At Fairmount, Jesse met Ruth Solomon. Ruth had also been born and raised in a southern sharecropper's family and had moved north with her parents. Jesse and Ruth had a lot in common.

(Above) **Fairmount Junior High School**

JESSE AND RILEY

Fairmount was also where Jesse first took part in team sports. Life in the open Alabama air and his love of running had given him speed and stamina (the energy to run for long periods). In gym class, the exercises strengthened his legs and his lungs. Charles Riley taught the gym class and led the Fairmount track team. He introduced himself to Jesse. "I'd noticed him watching me for a year or so," Jesse recalled. "Especially when we'd play games where there was running or jumping."

Riley saw that Jesse had the natural talent to do well in events such as the high jump and broad jump (later called the long jump). He encouraged Jesse to train harder than he would for regular gym classes. But Jesse had to work after school. So they agreed to start regular workouts before school.

Riley carefully coached Jesse on his running style. He taught the boys on his team to run as lightly as possible. He wanted them to keep their arms, heads, and chests steady while they ran. Look straight ahead, the coach suggested, and focus on the finish line, not on the other runners.

IT'S A FACT!

Riley and Jesse met every day on the sidewalk outside Fairmount for before-school workouts. After Jesse broke his first running record, Riley nicknamed him his "sidewalk champion."

Then Riley coached Jesse to get ready for competitions. He had Jesse run lengths that were longer than the sprints, or short races, he would actually have to race. After running for a quarter of a mile (440 yards), Jesse would have an easier time competing in the shorter races. These included the 220-yard, 200-yard, and 100-yard dashes.

Riley's advice greatly helped Jesse. So did Jesse's nearly perfect runner's body. He was slender, with strong but not bulky leg muscles. Photographs show that Owens ran with ease, while his opponents seemed to struggle.

An Olympic Dream

Charles Riley also guided Jesse outside of school. The young, promising athlete and the experienced coach became great friends. They shared meals together. They even hung out with one another in their spare time. Riley never said much. When he spoke, he often talked in stories or riddles. "Charles Riley was the kind of man who would say something to you when he wanted to, and only then," Jesse later said. But Riley's stories always carried an important point. He thought winning came from inner determination. He felt that the best athletes–the winners–overcome

Coach Charles Riley (left) was like a father to Jesse (right).

the desire to ease off when the going gets hard. As Riley often told Jesse, "Run to beat yourself."

With his hard training and Riley's guidance, Jesse built up the muscles in his legs. He became one of the best school athletes in Cleveland. After one year of Riley's coaching, Jesse was clocking just 11 seconds flat in the 100-yard dash. His marks began showing up in the record books. In 1928, he broke the world junior high school record in the high jump, at 6 feet, and in the broad jump, at 22 feet 11¾ inches.

That same year, Riley introduced Jesse to Charley Paddock, a world-famous track star. He had competed in the Summer Olympic Games in

Paris, France, in 1924. Jesse listened, while Paddock talked about competing in foreign places. Runners from all over the world had raced in the Summer Olympic Games in 1920 and 1924. After his meeting with Paddock, Jesse dreamed of making the U.S. Olympic team.

GOING TO EAST TECH

Jesse remained in school, training hard with Charles Riley. The rest of his family worked. Henry Owens and his other sons had jobs in a Cleveland steel mill. Jesse's sisters worked as maids and laundresses. Still, life was better in Cleveland than it had been in

As many as a dozen family members lived in the Owenses' duplex house. On the porch sit two sisters, two nieces, Jesse's mother, and his brother.

Oakville. The family had enough food to eat and better clothes to wear. And Jesse was still friends with Ruth Solomon.

Jesse's mother, Emma, was sure they had done the right thing by moving north to Cleveland. For Jesse's father, Henry, however, one bad thing seemed to follow another. He had never learned to read or write. So he was stuck with poor-paying jobs. One day in 1929, he was struck by a taxicab and injured. After the accident, he could not find steady work.

In the fall of 1930, Jesse enrolled at East Technical High School. Students at East Tech prepared for jobs instead of for college. They could take courses in auto mechanics, masonry (stonework), and other practical subjects. But by 1930, Jesse Owens was concentrating on another career–running.

Edgar Weil, the East Tech track coach, figured out that Jesse needed careful training. He invited Charles Riley to come to the school in the afternoons and continue training Jesse. Meanwhile, Jesse's relationship with Ruth became more serious.

By then, Jesse was the best-known young runner in the entire city. By his junior year, he was the star at every meet, or competition, he entered.

Edgar Weil *(right)* coaches Jesse *(second from right)* and his East Tech track teammates.

In the spring of 1932, Jesse's coaches were preparing him for his biggest challenge yet. They wanted him to try out for the U.S. Olympic team. The Summer Olympic Games would be held later that year in Los Angeles, California.

The American Olympic Association wanted to choose the best athletes for the U.S. team. The association held tryouts in different regions of the country. That year, the Midwest tryouts took place at Northwestern University in Evanston, Illinois.

THE STORY OF THE OLYMPIC GAMES

More than 2,700 years ago—in 776 B.C.—ancient Greeks held the first Olympic Games. The Greeks lived along the Mediterranean Sea. At that long-ago time, the cities of ancient Greece were often battling one another for power. But every four years, they stopped all their battles for a while and sent their best athletes to Olympia, a valley in southwestern Greece.

The Greeks held a religious festival in Olympia. The festival featured events of athletic strength and skill. The oldest event at the Olympia festival, or Olympic Games, was a footrace. The Greeks later added boxing, wrestling, discus throwing, and javelin throwing to the Olympics. Winners were admired throughout Greece.

About 2,200 years ago—in 197 B.C.—the Romans conquered the Greeks. The Romans lived in the center of the Mediterranean region, and they let the Games go on. Athletes from all over the Mediterranean region began competing. But about 1,600 years ago—in A.D. 394—the Roman emperor Theodosius stopped the Olympic Games. He was a Christian. He banned the Games because they were part of a religious festival that wasn't Christian.

In the late 1800s, a wealthy Frenchman named Baron Pierre de Coubertin brought back the ancient Games. The new, modern Olympics, Coubertin believed, would be a way for the different countries of the world to compete peacefully on the athletic field. He wanted the world to have a different way to fight than on a battlefield. The first modern Olympics were held in Athens, the capital of Greece, in 1896. These first modern Games were Summer Games. The first Winter Olympic Games took place in 1924 in Chamonix, France.

Jesse Owens competed in three events. He was part of the 100-meter and 200-meter dashes and the broad jump. He was already close to Olympic records in these events. He let the pressure of competing against the best athletes in the country make him nervous. He was beaten by Ralph Metcalfe, a more experienced runner from Marquette University, and by Eddie Tolan from the University of Michigan. Jesse wasn't part of the team at the 1932 Summer Games.

IT'S A FACT!

In international competition, the standard short sprints were the 100-meter and 200-meter dashes. These races are slightly longer versions of the American sprints.

FAMILY AND COMPETITION

Jesse was disappointed in his performance at the tryouts. Yet he began to see that he could compete with the best athletes in the country. He proved it a few weeks later. After the Los Angeles Games, an Olympic track squad came to Cleveland for a public competition. Jesse took part in it too. This time, Jesse won both the 100-meter and 200-meter sprints. He took second place in the broad jump behind Edward Gordon.

As it turned out, Owens had faced the toughest competition in the world that summer. At the Los Angeles Games, Tolan and Metcalfe had finished first and second in the 100-meter dash. They had placed first and third in the 200-meter race. Gordon had won the gold medal in the broad jump.

That same summer, another important event took place in Jesse's life. His daughter, Gloria, was born. Jesse and Ruth had become parents,

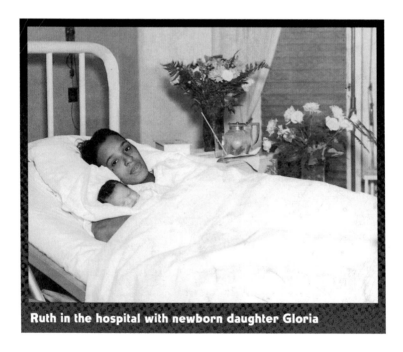

Ruth in the hospital with newborn daughter Gloria

Jesse fills a car with oil at his job as a gas station attendant.

even though they weren't married. Although the couple had a child, Ruth continued to live with her father and mother. They helped her take care of the new baby. Jesse helped support his daughter and Ruth. To earn money, Jesse took a job at a gas station in Cleveland. Ruth dropped out of school to work in a beauty parlor.

CHAPTER 3

SCHOOL SENSATION

JESSE STRUGGLED TO SUPPORT his young family. But his career on the running track was going smoothly. During his senior year at East Tech, he won every event he entered. He broke several national records. Crowds cheered him loudly. The track squad elected him captain.

In the spring of 1933, Ohio State University in Columbus, Ohio, held a high school track meet. Jesse broke the national high school broad jump record by three inches. He jumped 24 feet 3¾ inches. In June, he competed in the National Interscholastic Championships in Chicago, Illinois. At this meet, he set a new world record of 20.7 seconds in the 220-yard dash. At the same competition, Jesse ran the 100-yard dash in 9.4 seconds to tie the world record.

East Tech easily won the event. Cleveland proudly threw Jesse and the team a victory parade for the big win in Chicago.

COMPETING IN COLLEGE

In the meantime, Jesse had graduated from high school. Even though his grades weren't the best, he had tremendous athletic talent. So he faced an important decision. Where should he go to college?

Jesse had always struggled to keep up with his schoolwork. But his great athletic ability brought him the attention of several Big Ten universities. These schools—such as the University of Michigan and the University of Minnesota—belonged to the biggest and the best athletic conference in the country. No athletic scholarships were available in the 1930s. But Jesse and other poor athletes could count on a paying job. School officials set up these jobs to help their athletes pay for expenses.

Jesse and Riley drove north to the University of Michigan. They were there to meet the school's track coaches. The Michigan coaches very much wanted Jesse Owens on their team. A better offer for Jesse soon came from Ohio State University. And that's where Jesse wanted to go.

Jesse's high school grades were poor. But in the summer of 1933, he passed a series of exams that allowed him to enter college. He moved to Columbus to start classes in the fall of 1933. The university arranged for him to work part-time operating a freight elevator.

COLLEGE STANDOUT

Jesse was a college freshman in the fall of 1933. College rules said that he couldn't yet be a member of Ohio State's varsity track team. In practices, however, the young coach, Larry Snyder, put Jesse through hard training.

Snyder had Jesse cut back on the movement of his arms and hands. Snyder believed his motions were slowing him down. Snyder also had Jesse place his feet closer together at the starting line. The coach believed this new position would help Jesse react faster to the sound of the starter's gun.

The Amateur Athletic Union (AAU) saw Jesse's natural talent. It awarded him a spot on its All-American team, before he had even taken part in a single college track meet. In the spring of 1934, Jesse

Although Larry Snyder (left) recognized Jesse's skills as an athlete, he still felt Jesse could improve.

competed in an AAU event in New York. At this meet, he ran a close second place to Ralph Metcalfe in the 100-meter dash.

College rules said Jesse couldn't yet compete for the varsity team in meets against other colleges. But he could participate in public meets. At one of these meets, the judges let Jesse take a running start in the 100-yard dash. This meant he was already running when he crossed the starting line. He crossed the finish line in just 8.4 seconds. This time has never been equaled by any runner with a standing start (when the runner starts at the starting line).

Jesse's new job as an elevator operator gave him plenty of time to study. He worked only in the evenings, when cleaning crews used the elevators. Jesse sat at a desk near the elevator and tried to keep up with his studies. Nevertheless, he soon fell behind. By his sophomore year, Jesse was in danger of failing at Ohio State.

IT'S A FACT!

In the 1930s, runners ready to start a race dug their feet into the ground. They quickly jumped forward at the sound of the starter's gun. In later years, sprinters were able to use starting blocks. Runners set their feet in the blocks and pushed off against them. Starting blocks gave runners an easier and quicker start in a race.

Later in 1934, Jesse got a new job. He became a page, or messenger, for Ohio's state legislature in Columbus. The legislature made Ohio's laws. He worked when the state's legislators, or lawmakers, were at work. He delivered messages and helped with other office duties. The new job had more importance and paid more money.

ON THE TEAM

Jesse finally joined Ohio State's varsity track team in the spring of 1935. Larry Snyder worked with Jesse nearly every day. He put him through thousands of practice starts.

Both men knew that the start of any short-distance sprint was very important. The runner had to leap into motion in a split second. He could not hesitate or stumble. Snyder taught Jesse

Coach Snyder believed Jesse could improve his sprinting time by working on his start.

to crouch lower. The coach wanted Jesse to get more spring out of his legs at the start.

Jesse's first varsity meet was against the University of Indiana. He won three events. He placed second in his fourth event, the 70-yard low hurdles.

He competed in his first Big Ten finals at Ferry Field in Ann Arbor, Michigan, on May 25, 1935. Before this meet, he had been suffering from a sore back. Coach Snyder nearly benched him. "I'd hurt my back fooling around, wrestling with some friends," Jesse recalled. "It hurt so much I could barely bend down to start the first event. But once I started to compete, I forgot about it."

Jesse amazed everyone at the Ann Arbor meet. He won the 220-yard dash in 20.3 seconds. In just one try, he nailed the broad jump to a mark of 26 feet 8¼ inches. He ran the 220-yard low hurdles in 22.6 seconds. Each one of these marks was a new world record!

IT'S A FACT!

After the Ann Arbor meet, Jesse's teammates elected him captain of the team. This was the first time an African American was captain of any athletic team in the Big Ten.

(These times were also new world records in international contests—the 200-meter dash and 200-meter low hurdles.) In the 100-yard dash, Jesse missed another record by just one-tenth of a second. His official finishing time of 9.4 seconds tied the world record.

Many sportswriters believe that Jesse's 1935 Ann Arbor meet was the highlight of his entire athletic career. Some call it one of the greatest single showings in track history.

Snyder's coaching and Charles Riley's encouragement had Jesse running in his best form ever. He seemed a cinch to make the Olympic team in 1936.

UPS AND DOWNS

Even with athletic ability and growing fame, Jesse Owens still experienced academic problems, poverty, and racial discrimination (prejudice). Ohio State University and other colleges at the time did not treat blacks equally. While Jesse attended the school, only about one hundred of the fourteen thousand students were African Americans.

Because he was black, Jesse was not allowed to live on campus. Whites and blacks living together was against the rules. Instead, he had to live off campus in a boardinghouse with other African American students.

"Many blacks were not permitted in restaurants along High Street," remembered Jesse's teammate Charles Beetham. "They were not permitted in the theaters. In fact about the only place they could eat . . . was in restaurants on the campus." The discrimination was worse when the team traveled. "We had to make arrangements ahead of time for where we would stop to eat," Beetham said. "[Blacks] could not eat in the coffee shop or in the restaurants in the hotel where they stayed. They had to eat in their rooms." It was even worse in southern states. Southern colleges strictly banned blacks from any athletic competition with whites.

In the summer of 1935, Jesse and Ohio State's track team traveled to California. With all of his world-record performances, Jesse had become the track star to see. Newspapers printed stories about his life on and off the track.

On the track, Jesse won ten events in a row. Off the track, he struck up a friendship with a woman named Quincella Nickerson. Photographs showed her and Jesse together. Rumors went around that they were engaged. When Ruth Solomon heard the rumors, she became angry. She wrote Jesse a letter, then telephoned him. Jesse rushed back to Cleveland. He and Ruth were married the same day he returned home, on July 5, 1935, at the home of Ruth's parents.

Jesse and Ruth were married at her parents' home in Cleveland.

IT'S A FACT!

Jesse remembered that Ruth watched him change from a skinny kid into a track champion. She hung in there with him through the triumphs and the hard times.

After Jesse's marriage, track events continued to take him away from home. Restless by nature, Jesse liked constant travel. On top of it all, the 1936 Olympic Games were fast approaching. He was already favored to bring home some gold medals.

CHAPTER 4
MORE THAN THE OLYMPICS

IN THE SUMMER OF **1935**, Jesse was given a new job. He became an honorary page for a committee in the Ohio legislature. The job paid twenty-one dollars a week. But the legislature didn't meet in the summer, so Jesse didn't have any specific duties. Instead, he was free to train, travel, and compete. Jesse collected and spent money from the state government without ever going to the state capitol in Columbus.

(Above) **Jesse trained hard to win a spot on the U.S. Olympic team.**

A NEAR MISS

The money and the free time helped him. But his position as an honorary page also nearly kept him from going to the 1936 Olympics. The AAU had a lot of influence with the American Olympic Association. AAU athletes could not earn money for taking part in athletic competitions. Nor could they get money through awards, prizes, or honorary jobs. To AAU officials, Jesse seemed to be getting money because of his ability on the running track. The $159 he had earned from a no-show job as a page looked like an illegal athletic scholarship. In August 1935, the AAU decided to look into the matter.

Jesse had to go to Cleveland to explain. Many of the AAU officials who listened understood his situation. Jesse's family had no money to support him. He needed as much time as possible to remain in shape for competition. Several Ohio State officials spoke up for their star runner. As a result, the AAU decided in Jesse's favor. He could return to amateur (nonpaid) sports. Meanwhile, Jesse decided to return the money he had earned as an honorary page. He didn't want anything to get in the way of going to the Olympics.

Things looked like they were getting back to normal. But then Jesse's poor grades forced him to stop being part of the track team. He had to practice on his own. This change didn't bother Jesse. He knew three years had passed since his last try for the Olympic team. But Jesse also knew he was faster, better trained, and more confident. If he could make the team, he'd have a good chance to compete against the world's best runners and athletes.

HITLER AND THE NAZIS

Jesse didn't yet realize there would be much more to the 1936 Games than athletic events. Back in the spring of 1932, the International Olympic Committee (IOC) had decided to hold the 1936 Olympic Games in Germany. The Winter Games would take place in the mountains of southern Germany. The Summer Games would take place in the German capital of Berlin.

Adolf Hitler and his Nazi Party had taken power in 1933. They had been preparing for the 1936 Olympic Games ever since. Hitler saw the Games as a chance to show the world that Nazi ideas were a success. He also saw the Games as a way for German athletes to prove his theories about the superiority of the German people.

Germany had banned Jewish athletes from Germany's amateur sporting clubs. The members of these clubs were the only athletes allowed to try out for the German Olympic team. The Nazi government stopped German Jews from participating in any organized team sport.

Jesse Owens may not have thought much about Adolf Hitler or the Nazi Party as he prepared to qualify for the U.S. Olympic team. But many other people were giving Hitler attention. Many

LIFE IN NAZI GERMANY

Adolf Hitler and his Nazi Party took complete control of Germany's economy, education, and the media. The party had power over nearly every part of Germany's culture, including athletics. People who disagreed with Hitler were fired, sent to prison, or forced to leave the country.

Hitler believed Germans and other white northern Europeans were physically and mentally better than other groups around the world. His ideas won support among Germans because they were unhappy with the peace treaty after World War 1. Hitler wrote that certain people within Germany, particularly German Jews, had caused the defeat. Hitler was determined to rid Germany of all Jews. After taking power, the Nazis forced many German Jews out of their jobs and their homes. Jews began leaving the country by the thousands. Many who stayed were sent to prison.

firmly believed that the United States should boycott, or refuse to attend, the 1936 Games. They felt the boycott was a way to protest Hitler's racist and anti-Jewish ideas and actions.

BOYCOTT?

Avery Brundage was the president of the American Olympic Association. He liked the idea of a U.S. boycott. But others opposed it. They believed that racial discrimination was just as bad in the United States as it was in Germany. They saw no reason to take away the chance for young athletes to disprove Hitler's racist ideas. Some opposed the boycott because they thought the United States shouldn't get involved in Germany's affairs.

Germany then announced that a group of German Jewish athletes would be allowed to take

IT'S A FACT!

Avery Brundage competed as a track athlete in the 1912 Summer Olympics in Stockholm, Sweden. After graduating from college, he kept up his interest in amateur athletics. He became president of the American Olympic Committee in 1928. He served as IOC president from 1952 to 1972.

part in Olympic training. Brundage decided to go to
Germany and judge things for himself. He toured the
country and met with several German Jewish leaders,
who were always with Nazi officials. Brundage was
impressed by the country's wealth and how well
things were run. German leaders convinced him that
their anti-Jewish ideas had changed.

After his tour, Brundage decided that Hitler
was following the Olympic rules. He thought that
the United States should send a team to the Games.
In late 1935, the AAU also changed its mind and
withdrew from the boycott. Yet in September 1935,
Germany passed anti-Jewish laws. The laws stripped
Jewish athletes and ordinary Jewish citizens of their
right to protection under German laws.

MAKING THE TEAM

Political tension went on into late 1935, but Jesse
kept running, jumping, and winning. "I wanted no
part of politics," he wrote later. "The purpose of the
Olympics, anyway, was to do your best." By that
time, his grades had improved because he studied
harder. In the spring of 1936, he rejoined Ohio
State's track team. He could again take part in Big
Ten competitions.

On May 16, 1936, at the University of
Wisconsin at Madison, he set a new world record
in the 100-yard dash. His time was 9.3 seconds. A
week later, he was on his home track at Ohio State.
Jesse won all four events he entered. He was
running at peak form. Word of his ability quickly
spread overseas. Fans and sportswriters were
looking forward to seeing what twenty-two-year-old
Jesse could do in Berlin.

Ralph Metcalfe and Eulace Peacock were
Jesse's toughest competition at the Olympic tryouts.

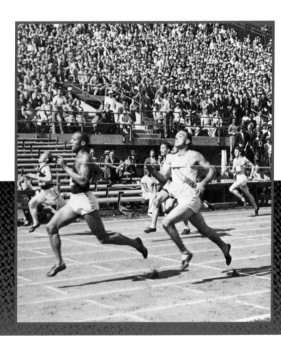

After earning
back his spot on
the Ohio State
track team, Jesse
*(second runner
from the left)* won
race after race.

Metcalfe already held three Olympic medals from the 1932 Games in Los Angeles. "Ralph was tall, yet powerful," Jesse wrote, "with legs longer and more heavily muscled than mine, a chest with more lung capacity." At the Olympic tryout finals, Owens and Metcalfe easily made the team. Jesse won all three of his events—the 100-meter dash, the 200-meter dash, and the broad jump. Peacock suffered an injury and didn't make the team.

Owens and Metcalfe were two of nineteen African American athletes to qualify for the 1936 U.S. Olympic team. Ten were on the men's track team. Two were on the women's track squad. Other African Americans were on the boxing and weightlifting teams.

CHAPTER 5

GOING TO BERLIN

IN 1936, THE GREAT DEPRESSION was
still making life difficult worldwide. The 382-
member Olympic team had to find ways to pay
expenses to get to the Games.

Baron Pierre de Coubertin had set strict
standards about money and amateur athletes.
Olympic athletes could not earn money from athletic
contests of any kind. The AAU and the American
Olympic Association made sure the Olympic athletes
didn't break, or even bend, the rules.

The American Olympic Association asked for
money from groups such as the AAU and the
National Collegiate Athletic Association (NCAA). In
turn, the NCAA asked its member schools to send
funds. But money came in slowly and was less than
expected. The AAU wanted to make sure the team's

bills would be paid. It scheduled several track-and-field public exhibition meets in Europe just after the Olympic Games. The AAU was sure the U.S. team would do well in Berlin. AAU officials thought large crowds would come to see Jesse Owens and his teammates perform after the Games.

GETTING READY

Jesse probably did not give the post-Olympic events much thought. He and the rest of the team boarded the passenger ship SS *Manhattan* on July

Some of Jesse's teammates aboard the SS *Manhattan* (from left to right): Jimmy LuValle, Archie Williams, John Woodruff, Ben Johnson, and Mack Robinson

15, 1936, for the voyage across the Atlantic Ocean to Europe. Larry Snyder also took the trip, although he had to pay his own way. The trip lasted nine days through rough seas and stormy weather. Jesse and several other members of the team had seasickness.

For the most part, though, Jesse enjoyed the voyage. It was the first time he had ever been on a ship. His easygoing manner attracted strangers. He signed hundreds of autographs for fans as well as teammates. On July 24, 1936, the *Manhattan* docked at the German port of Bremerhaven. The team reached Berlin by express train. All the international athletes were given a tour of the huge facilities prepared for the Games. The largest of the nine arenas was the gigantic Olympic Stadium. It could hold 110,000 spectators. The track-and-field events would be held there.

IT'S A FACT!

At the end of the voyage, the team voted Jesse the best-dressed athlete. He came in second for most popular athlete, behind distance runner Glenn Cunningham.

CREATING AN OLYMPIC VILLAGE

German architects had designed the first Olympic Village a few miles west of Berlin. The village had 160 separate cottages. Each housed twenty-four male athletes. (Women were housed in a large dormitory building.) Athletes could enjoy a library, a theater, practice fields, and a swimming pool. Doctors, dentists, and barbers were on hand. A guide who spoke the team's language lived in each cottage.

German officials came up with a color-coded system to tell athletes where they were to stay and when they would eat. Codes said when buses would take them to their events. The Berlin Olympic Village served as a model for later Olympic villages.

Hitler had closely looked over Germany's preparations for the Games. His orders were to give the world a good impression of Germany. He wanted no obvious anti-Jewish activity. For example, the government temporarily stopped arresting Germans who opposed Nazism.

The Games opened on Saturday, August 1. Thousands of soldiers, schoolchildren, and bands marched through the streets and into the stadium as part of the ceremony. Hitler watched as a flaming torch lit the Olympic fire. More than three thousand runners had relayed the torch, turn by turn, from the ruins of Olympia in Greece to Germany. It was the

The last runner brings the Olympic flame from Olympia, Greece, to Berlin for the 1936 Games.

first time the torch had been relayed to the opening ceremonies. The national teams marched around the track. Each team held up its nation's flag.

SNUBS BY HITLER

Sunday, August 2, was the first day of competition. That day, a member of the German team, Hans Woellke, won the shot-put competition. Woellke was the first German to win an Olympic track-and-field event. He went through the victory ceremony. Then Hitler invited Woellke to come to his box to receive his personal congratulations. Later, three athletes from Finland took first, second, and third place in the 10,000-meter run. German women took gold and silver medals in the javelin throw. All received Hitler's personal congratulations.

The main event of the first day was the high jump. Cornelius Johnson, an African American on the U.S. team, won the event with a jump of 7 feet 6¼ inches. But Hitler left his box and the stadium without congratulating Johnson.

The IOC president, Henri de Baillet-Latour, had warned Hitler that he must not show any favoritism. That meant either all gold medalists should receive his congratulations or none should. Hitler decided none would.

On the same day, Jesse was scheduled to compete in the preliminary heats, or contests, for the 100-meter dash. There were twelve elimination heats for the sixty-eight people in the races. Those who survived the heats would then be in a series of four quarterfinals and semifinals that same afternoon. In the last preliminary race, Jesse ran the sprint in 10.3 seconds. His mark tied the Olympic record.

THE FIRST GOLD

The 100-meter finals took place the next day, on August 3. A storm had passed through earlier in the day. The inside track–Jesse's lane–was soft and muddy. Before starting the race, the judges moved the entire field one lane to the right. They didn't want the soft conditions to put any runner at a disadvantage.

Jesse took his starting position alongside Ralph Metcalfe and Frank Wykoff of the United States. Erich Borchmeyer of Germany, Lennart Strandberg of Sweden, and Martinus Osendarp of the Netherlands were in the other lanes. The starter raised his gun. The audience waited. They were expecting to see a spectacular race and perhaps even a new record. "I was looking

IT'S A FACT!

The inside track is the one closest to the inside of a curved racetrack. The runner who has won the semifinal race gets to run in the inside track in the finals. This runner doesn't have a person running on both sides as a distraction. This can be an advantage. So the term "having the inside track" usually means having an advantage of some sort.

only at the finish line and realizing that five of the world's fastest humans wanted to beat me to it," Jesse later said.

When the gun sounded, Jesse took the lead immediately. Metcalfe stumbled and fell behind the pack. Then he began passing the others. As the runners approached the finish line, Metcalfe passed Osendarp. He was gaining on Jesse. But Jesse was still about one meter in front of Metcalfe, who came in second. Osendarp came in third. Wykoff, Borchmeyer, and Strandberg held the last three places. The winning time was 10.3 seconds, again tying the Olympic record.

Jesse (right) crosses the finish line to win the 100-meter, his first gold medal.

More than 100,000 people rose to their feet. They cheered as Jesse Owens jogged around the track for a victory lap. Hitler watched and listened. The crowd was chanting Jesse's name. He had won his first Olympic gold medal. In just 10.3 seconds, Jesse Owens had become the star of the 1936 Olympic Games.

6 MAKING OLYMPIC HISTORY

THE NEXT DAY, AUGUST 4, Jesse ran in two preliminaries for the 200-meter dash. These heats would decide the runners for the August 5 semifinal races. The track had dried out. The improved track helped Jesse to run both races in 21.1 seconds, a new world record.

(Above) Jesse was feeling confident after winning his first Olympic gold medal.

The broad jump preliminaries also took place on the afternoon of August 4. Jesse was favored to win the event. After all, he already held the world record of 26 feet 8¼ inches. But he first needed to qualify for the finals. He had to reach or go farther than 23 feet 5½ inches. Jesse was confident. He had been passing that mark since high school.

Jesse began warming up on the inside field. He jogged along the track to get the feel of the ground and the takeoff board. He took a short practice run across the broad jump pit. Suddenly, a judge sent up a red flag. Jesse's practice run had been counted as one of his three tries! In his first official Olympic broad jump, Jesse Owens had not even left the ground.

On the second try, Jesse made sure to take a jump. But his foot touched beyond the front edge of the takeoff board. This is considered a foul or a scratch. The judges raised the red flag once again. Jesse's jump didn't count. He had only one try left to qualify for the broad jump finals. This time, he gave himself plenty of room behind the takeoff board, planted solidly, and jumped just one-half inch past the qualifying mark.

IT'S A FACT!

After Jesse fouled on his second try, he was in danger of not making the finals at all. The German long jumper Luz Long introduced himself to Jesse. Long suggested that Jesse start his run farther back. With more running speed, he would be sure to qualify safely. Jesse took Long's advice. Both athletes went on to the finals.

Sixteen athletes took part in the finals of the broad jump. Jesse was the favorite. His strongest competition came from the German athlete Luz Long. To many onlookers, the head-to-head contest between Jesse and Long was like a test of the Nazi ideas of racial superiority. Long was tall and blond, a perfect German. Jesse was black. The Nazis considered blacks "primitive" and "subhuman." The two men jumped nearly equal marks in the first try of the finals. On the second, Owens jumped just over 26 feet. This was the first time in history that an Olympic athlete had gone beyond 26 feet in the broad jump.

The two athletes continued. They nearly matched one another through several more tries. In all, Long and Owens tied the Olympic record once and beat it five times. On his last jump, Jesse leaped an

Jesse won a gold medal for this broad jump at the Berlin Olympics. He also set a world record.

Luz Long's broad jump was good—but not good enough to beat Jesse.

amazing 26 feet 5⁵⁄₁₆ inches. This was a new Olympic record. "I decided I wasn't going to come down," Jesse remembered. "I was going to stay up in the air forever."

Long had fouled on his next-to-last jump. On his last jump, he only made 25 feet 9¾ inches. This was still better than the old Olympic record but not enough to beat Jesse. Long rushed up to Jesse and immediately congratulated him on the victory. The two men walked off the field together. From that moment on, they remained friends.

THE 200-METER DASH

The rainy weather continued as Jesse prepared for his last event—the 200-meter finals. He had easily qualified for the race. He had won his semifinal heat with a time of 21.3 seconds. This time was just one-tenth of a second slower than the Olympic record. But Jesse knew he would probably have to do better than that. His own teammate Mack Robinson was his main competition.

The finals of the 200-meter dash took place on August 5. The competitors were Owens, Robinson, Martinus Osendarp and Wijnand van Beveren of the Netherlands, Paul Hänni of Switzerland, and Lee Orr of Canada. But from the instant the starting gun sounded, Jesse Owens ran well ahead of the field. He crossed the finish line three meters ahead of Robinson and Osendarp. His effort shattered the old Olympic and world records with a time of 20.7 seconds. It was Jesse's third gold medal.

IT'S A FACT!

Mack Robinson was the older brother of a rising young athlete named Jackie Robinson. Jackie would later be the first African American to play in Major League Baseball.

A FINAL GOLD

Jesse hoped to spend the rest of the Olympic Games resting, watching, and signing autographs.

But to his surprise, he was entered in one more
race. On August 7, the coach of the 400-meter
relay team, Dean Cromwell, picked Jesse and
Ralph Metcalfe to run in place of Sam Stoller and
Marty Glickman.

Stoller and Glickman happened to be the only
two Jewish athletes on the U.S. track-and-field team.
They had come to Berlin to compete. But if they
won a medal, they'd also show up Hitler. By this
time, Hitler's anti-Jewish views were well known.
But Coach Cromwell had suddenly changed the
lineup to Owens, Foy Draper, Frank Wykoff, and
Ralph Metcalfe. Stoller
and Glickman were off the
relay team.

The decision stunned
every member of the U.S.
track-and-field team.
Glickman reacted angrily.
He pointed out that any
four runners from the
team would probably win the relay. Marty
Glickman later remembered that Jesse protested
the decision. "Coach, let Marty and Sam run,"
Jesse said. "I've had enough. I've won three gold

IT'S A FACT!

**In 1998, the U.S.
Olympic Committee
publicly apologized
for its decision to
replace the athletes
in 1936.**

medals. Let them run. They deserve it." The coach told Jesse to run anyway.

Writers and athletes still argue over Cromwell's reasons for dropping Stoller and Glickman from the relay team. Cromwell told the team that the Germans had saved their best runners for the relay race. Adding Owens and Metcalfe, he believed, would give the U.S. squad its best chance of winning. Others believe Dean Cromwell wanted Draper and Wykoff on the team because the two runners attended the University of Southern California, where Cromwell coached. Glickman believed Cromwell simply acted out of anti-Semitism (prejudice against Jews). He wanted to save Adolf Hitler the embarrassment of seeing his team beaten by a squad that included Jewish runners.

On the morning of August 8, the new U.S. relay team ran the semifinal race in 40 seconds. This time equaled the world-record time. That afternoon, in the finals, Jesse Owens ran the first leg of the 100 meters. His great speed gave the team a lead of 5 meters. He passed the baton to Ralph Metcalfe, who also ran well. Metcalfe added 2 meters to the lead. Draper and Wykoff finished

Jesse helped the U.S. relay team win a gold medal and break records.

the relay with the U.S. team 15 meters ahead of second-place Italy. The squad had set a new world record time of 39.8 seconds. This mark would stand for twenty years.

MAKING HISTORY

Jesse Owens carried away four gold medals. This amount was three more than any other track athlete in Berlin had won. It was more than anyone else had won to that point in Olympic track history. He also set three new world records.

Germany won the overall medals, with a total of thirty-three gold medals. The United States, which finished in second place, stood out in the track-and-field events. Also, with the entire world watching, Jesse Owens's performance had shown Hitler's theories on race to be nonsense.

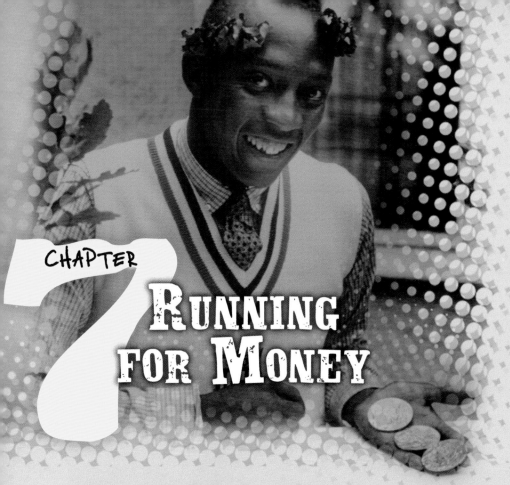

CHAPTER 7
RUNNING FOR MONEY

AFTER THE 1936 OLYMPICS, Jesse Owens packed his bags. He was signing autographs and posing for photographs. He was ready for the voyage home. He had nearly forgotten that the U.S. track team still had work to do. The AAU had scheduled the team for several exhibition meets after the Berlin Games. So instead of sailing back across the Atlantic Ocean, Jesse boarded planes and trains for shorter trips across Europe.

(Above) Jesse poses with three of his medals. He is wearing laurel leaves around his head. The ancient Greeks gave laurel leaves to the winners at the first Olympic Games.

The first stop was Cologne, in western Germany. At this first exhibition, Ralph Metcalfe edged out Jesse in the 100-meter dash. The next day, the team boarded an early morning flight for Prague, Czechoslovakia. Jesse ran that evening. He then boarded another train for Bochum, Germany. He ran the following day. The day after that, he was in London, England. He prepared for more sprints, broad jumps, photographs, interviews, autographs, and crowds.

British boys run with Jesse during a workout.

The tough competition at the Olympics had already drained Jesse physically. He couldn't hope to match the marks he had made in Berlin. His family was back home. He was receiving lots of job offers. Some of them paid well for the time. Jesse had trouble focusing on his events. He felt a growing resentment at being shown off like a prize-winning horse.

After reaching London, Jesse competed in a 400-meter relay race. Then, at a press conference, he declared, "I'm burned out, I'm busted, and I'm tired of being treated like cattle. I know how hard it is for a member of my race to make money... and I have to reach for it while it's being offered me."

The team was to continue on to Sweden for more exhibitions. Jesse had a long talk with Larry Snyder. He followed Snyder's advice and missed the plane to Sweden on purpose. Owens and Snyder boarded the passenger ship *Queen Mary* and returned to New York.

After Berlin

Skipping the rest of the tour turned out to be one of the most important decisions of Jesse's life. The leaders of the AAU were outraged. It immediately stopped Jesse from competing in AAU-sponsored events in the United States.

The AAU's decision may have worried Jesse. But he had other things to think about on the return voyage. He had already received offers from agents and stars in Hollywood and New York. Ohio State wanted Jesse to return and finish his college education. School officials were sure Jesse would be a big draw at the school's upcoming track meets.

Meanwhile, Cleveland had prepared a welcoming party to meet Jesse's train from New York. The Ohio city put on a victory parade. A grand celebration in front of Cleveland's City Hall was next. The mayor and other officials gave speeches of praise. Another parade wound through the streets of Columbus. The mayor and Ohio's governor personally greeted the world's fastest man. When the ship carrying the other members of the track team docked in New York, Jesse returned to the city to be with them. Jesse rode in the lead car of the motor parade. The team attended a medal ceremony hosted by New York's mayor, Fiorello La Guardia.

Hailed as the fastest man in the world, Jesse was honored in many parades.

At the same time, Jesse had to think carefully about his future. A college degree would help him land a good-paying job. On the other hand, he might never again have a chance to use his worldwide fame. Jesse decided to quit college for the time being. He wanted to take advantage of the offers that were coming his way.

In New York, Jesse signed a contract with an agent named Marty Forkins. Forkins would screen all the offers and negotiate all the contracts for

Jesse. Several large companies had already hired
Jesse to sell their products in print and on the
radio. Jesse also accepted paid offers to make
personal appearances and to speak at public events.

SUPPORTING POLITICIANS

Politicians also wanted Jesse Owens. As the best-
known athlete in the world, he could be a helpful
part of their campaigns. Like Olympic Games,
presidential elections come around every four
years. For the elections of 1936, both the
Democratic and Republican Parties wanted to use
Jesse Owens's famous name. They wanted to build
on his public support.

Politicians had never paid much attention to
athletes, especially to African American athletes. By
1936, things were beginning to change. For many
years, African Americans had voted for Republican
candidates. The Republican Party was the party of
President Abraham Lincoln. In the 1860s, Lincoln
had led the U.S. government to outlaw slavery.

During the Great Depression, Franklin
Roosevelt—a Democrat—was president. He and the
Democratic Party had made laws that had helped
unemployed, hungry, and desperate families, black

as well as white. Roosevelt was popular all over the country. Many people believed black voters would vote to reelect Roosevelt. For either party, Jesse Owens could help black voters make up their minds.

Jesse thought things over and decided to support the Republican candidate, Alf Landon. The Republican Party paid Jesse a lot of money for his support. In September and October of 1936, Jesse traveled all over the East and Midwest. He talked about the Berlin Olympic Games and the U.S.

Jesse didn't see much of Ruth while he was campaigning for Alf Landon.

presidential election. But in politics, Jesse didn't run quite as well as he did in the Olympics. Most voters, including most African Americans, sided with Franklin Roosevelt. He beat Landon easily.

MORE EXHIBITIONS

Despite his fame, Jesse still had no permanent job. He wanted to give his life more direction. While Jesse was campaigning for the Republican Party, Marty Forkins was making hundreds of telephone calls. He arranged for Jesse to endorse, or sell, products in newspapers and on the radio. He made appointments for Jesse to give speeches at ball games and banquets. Forkins talked with movie producers about landing Jesse a starring role in a Hollywood film. But the offers all turned out to be nothing more than empty promises. Jesse paid little attention.

Jesse's appearances were earning him more than he could have dreamed of earning before the Olympics. He bought a new car and a new house. He bought a fine house for his parents. He bought new clothes for himself and jewelry for Ruth. He made a down payment on a new car for Charles Riley.

Because Jesse was earning money while continuing to be an athlete, he was banned from amateur track meets. So he became a one-man running exhibition. It was the only way for him to make money as an athlete. No professional track teams or broad-jumping leagues existed at the time.

The exhibitions were partly an athletic event and partly a circus. Jesse ran against the fastest athletes in whatever town he was in. He also broad jumped and raced over low hurdles. He sometimes gave his competitors a head start of ten or twenty yards. At one exhibition in Chicago, he raced against heavyweight boxer Joe Louis.

A FAMOUS STUNT

Jesse once competed in a famous stunt during the halftime of a soccer match in Havana, Cuba. Jesse had been scheduled to race against Cuba's fastest human, Conrado Rodrigues. But the AAU threatened to take away Rodrigues's amateur standing in the United States. The Cuban sprinter backed out of the race.

Marty Forkins then arranged for Jesse to run against a Thoroughbred racehorse named Julio McCaw. Jesse had a forty-yard head start. He beat the horse by a few yards and earned two thousand dollars.

Jesse earned money from these appearances. But he also earned scorn from some writers and officials involved in amateur sports. Many of them disliked Jesse for profiting from his success at Berlin. For example, the Sullivan Committee made an annual award to the year's best amateur athlete. In 1936, the committee snubbed Jesse by voting him second place. Despite Jesse's record-setting performances in Berlin, the Sullivan Trophy went to Glenn Morris. He had won the Olympic decathlon, a ten-event competition.

MANY JOBS

Moneymaking offers for Jesse began to slow. In the winter of 1936–1937, he was looking for a more permanent job. In January 1937, Consolidated Radio Artists hired him to lead a twelve-piece dance band on a coast-to-coast tour. Jesse's job was to stand up in front of the band and announce each number. "They had me sing a little," Jesse recalled, "but that was a horrible mistake. I can't carry a tune in a bucket."

IT'S A FACT!

Eddie Cantor, a famous radio and stage comedian, offered Jesse forty thousand dollars to appear in a series of radio broadcasts.

In April 1937, Jesse quit the band. That fall, he started a professional basketball squad that he named the Olympians. The team traveled from city to city. They played against local amateur clubs as well as college teams. At halftime, Owens gave short talks and put on demonstrations of his running skill and speed. The team earned money and won most of its games. But it soon ran into trouble with the

Jesse *(kneeling)* **poses with an Olympians basketball team.**

AAU. According to AAU rules, any team that participated in amateur events could not profit from its touring. It could only make enough money to pay expenses. The AAU barred college squads from playing against the Olympians. In the spring of 1938, the squad was disbanded.

Jesse Owens decided to settle down in Cleveland with his growing family. He and Ruth had another daughter, Beverly. In the summer of 1938, he took a job as a playground director. That fall, he started a dry-cleaning business with

Jesse only had his dry-cleaning business for a few months before it ran into money problems.

two partners. But Jesse wasn't interested in the day-to-day details of running the Jesse Owens Dry Cleaning Company. In the fall and winter of 1938–1939, the company struggled to meet its many debts on loans and equipment.

BANKRUPTCY

In 1939, the Jesse Owens Dry Cleaning Company closed down. Jesse had only $2,050 in the bank. His debts came to $8,891. Jesse also owed money to the Internal Revenue Service (IRS, the government's tax-collection agency). The IRS discovered that Jesse had not paid income tax on $20,000 he had earned after the Berlin Olympics. Jesse, only twenty-five years old, filed for bankruptcy. This legal document says that a person has run out of money. A court decides how to pay off the debts. Sometimes property is sold to make money. Sometimes the bankrupt person pays off debts over time.

Jesse settled his bankruptcy case in Cleveland. Then he went back on the road to tour and earn money. In 1939, he traveled with the Indianapolis Clowns and the Toledo Crawfords. These baseball teams played in the midwestern and the southern states. At the end of each game, Jesse would put on a tracksuit and get ready to race. He'd race against the fastest man in town, giving his opponent a ten-yard lead. Jesse always won.

Jesse also kept racing against horses. Many years later, the memory left him sad and bitter. "I was no longer a proud man who had won four Olympic gold medals," he wrote. "I was a spectacle, a freak who made his living by competing–dishonestly–against dumb animals. I hated it."

He also experienced problems in his personal life. His long road trips often left his wife alone to care for their daughters. In March 1940, Jesse's mother died. Not long after, his father died of a heart attack. These setbacks were hard to get over.

TURNING POINTS

At the same time, people were beginning to forget about Jesse's accomplishments in the Olympic Games. His name had disappeared from the sports pages. By 1940, sports fans and sportswriters were beginning to look for another person to be the world's fastest human. Other athletes were

approaching and sometimes beating some of
Jesse's records.

Jesse decided that better-paying exhibitions or
starring roles in movies weren't going to fix his
declining fame. In 1940, he decided to return to
Columbus with his family, including another baby
daughter named Marlene. He reenrolled at Ohio
State to finish his studies and to earn his college
degree. While a student, he accepted a position as
an assistant coach with Ohio State's track team.

But Jesse couldn't concentrate on his studies.
After his first term, Jesse was expelled from Ohio
State for low grades. He was allowed to return for
the next term and try once more. He continued to
struggle with his classwork. Finally, in December
1941, he left Ohio State University for good. He
had never been able to keep up the minimum
grade point average needed to graduate.

That month was an important turning point
for Jesse Owens. It was also a turning point for
the rest of the world. On December 7, 1941, Japan
bombed the U.S. naval base at Pearl Harbor on
the Hawaiian island of Oahu. The United States
was suddenly at war with Japan and its ally,
Germany.

For Europe, World War II (1939–1945) had begun in September 1939. At that time, German armies had invaded Poland. By the spring of 1940, Germany had also taken over France, Belgium, and the Netherlands. Hitler's ally Japan invaded China, Southeast Asia, and the Philippines. The 1940 Olympic Games were supposed to be held in Tokyo, Japan. They were canceled before the start of the war. By 1942, the entire world seemed to be at war.

IT'S A FACT!

In ancient Greece, war stopped when each Olympics took place. In modern times, the Olympic Games stopped for war. The Olympic Games were canceled, during World War II, in 1940 and 1944.

AMERICA
CALLING

CHAPTER 8

place
se

THE WORLD'S FASTEST MANAGER

THE UNITED STATES officially entered
World War II on December 8, 1941, the day
after the attack on Pearl Harbor. U.S. military
rules didn't require the head of a family to serve
in the armed forces. So Jesse Owens wouldn't be
required to go into the military. But in January
1942, the U.S. government asked him to help
run a government fitness program. He gave
speeches on fitness and health. He helped start
exercise programs in African American

(Above)
**During
World War II,
the U.S.
government
hired Jesse.
He ran a
program that
encouraged
African
Americans
to stay
physically fit.**

communities across the country. While leading a fitness clinic in Detroit, Michigan, Jesse learned about a job opening with the Ford Motor Company.

LIFE WITH FORD

Ford and other U.S. car companies were building tanks, planes, guns, and spare parts for the war. All of these supplies were shipped to U.S. forces overseas. These companies had tough production schedules to meet. The Ford factories ran night and day. The company hired thousands of new laborers to work the extra shifts. Many of these new workers were African Americans. They had moved to Detroit from other cities in the Midwest and from the South.

Jesse became a personnel manager with Ford. He moved his family to Detroit.

Jesse never really felt comfortable at a desk job. He preferred to be active and to travel.

His job was to help oversee black workers at the company's various factories. He checked into the backgrounds of people looking for jobs. He fired workers when necessary. He also worked out problems between workers and bosses.

The job wasn't easy. Workers and bosses at Ford didn't always get along. The workers were well paid, but they sometimes got bored. Most of the workers were on an assembly line. Each worker on the line did exactly the same job every day. The Ford company also had strict rules. They caused stress and tiredness.

Jesse's strongest qualification for his new job was his easygoing and polite manner. He got along with most people. This trait eased the sometimes bitter words between workers and bosses. Jesse was soon promoted to be director of personnel for the black workers at Ford's River Rouge plant in Michigan. The company also asked him to serve as a spokesperson for the black community living in and around Detroit.

In 1945, Henry Ford II took over as president of the company. He was the grandson of the company's founder, Henry Ford. The Ford Motor Company had gained an image of being against the workers. Henry Ford II was determined to change Ford's poor image. He fired many managers and personnel directors. The company offered Jesse a lesser job in October 1945. Instead of accepting the change, however, Jesse turned it down. In turn, the company fired him.

More Public Appearances

Jesse seemed almost happy to leave his job at Ford. In fact, he wasn't very well suited for a big corporation like the Ford Motor Company. He disliked the stress of a day-to-day management job. Jesse had a restless nature and was sometimes impatient. He found it hard to concentrate on the same task. Instead, he loved to travel and to divide his time among many different projects at once. He also liked working alone. When he was in front of an audience, he depended only on his own ability. His enthusiasm often carried him through his talks.

World War II had ended in September 1945. The United States and the other nations fighting against Germany and Japan won. Soon after, thirty-two-year-old Jesse was traveling again with exhibition teams. He appeared with the Harlem

Globetrotters. They were a popular basketball team that performed stunts and jokes in front of large crowds. He also appeared with a baseball team called the Cincinnati Crescents. At the games, Jesse signed autographs. He talked to fans about his Olympic feats. He entertained audiences with his running exhibitions. Often his sprints nearly equaled his world-record times.

Jesse agreed to hundreds of public appearances. He often spent only a single night or even just a few hours in one place. The busy schedule was hard for his wife and growing daughters. Jesse was away from home for weeks at a time. Ruth Owens had to do her best to guide her three girls through childhood and school.

In 1949, Jesse decided to move from Detroit to Chicago. This decision meant his family would leave behind friends, schools, and a home. Gloria, Jesse's eldest daughter, decided to remain with family friends in Detroit while she finished her last year of high school.

In Chicago, Jesse found that his fame as an Olympic gold medalist opened up some job opportunities. Many different companies hired him to help sell their products. He started his own public relations business. He also spent time with charity groups such as the South Side Boys Club. He appeared on radio programs. He was the master of ceremonies, or host, at banquets, meetings, and sporting events. He also began writing a regular column for the *Chicago Defender*, an African American newspaper.

Jesse wrote about issues important to African Americans. These issues included education, job

Jesse worked with youth at the South Side Boys Club. Here, Jesse works with heavyweight boxing champion James T. Braddock.

opportunities, and justice under the law. By the 1950s, he had became a respected member of Chicago society. Many people, both black and white, were asking his opinion on issues.

GOODWILL AMBASSADOR

Jesse had already suffered his share of racial discrimination. He had seen outright racism as a young track athlete in high school and college. His victories at the Olympic Games had not given him a steady, good-paying job. But throughout his life, Jesse believed strongly in depending on yourself. He believed that all the people in the United States, regardless of their color or background, could achieve their dreams through hard work and not giving up.

Politicians and business leaders liked this positive message. It made their leadership in the United States look positive. As a result, Jesse remained in high demand for political campaigns.

In 1952, he publicly supported the Republican candidate for governor of Illinois. This support, in turn, earned political job appointments. In the next year, he was given a position as head of the Illinois State Athletic Commission. In this job, he traveled all over the state to oversee boxing matches. In

IT'S A FACT!

In his autobiography, Jesse wrote about a chat he had with the African American leader Martin Luther King Jr. in the 1950s. In their talk, Jesse told King about feeling a bit lost. King suggested finding a way to bring together Jesse's love of sports with his need to hold a good job. The job with the Illinois Youth Commission was the result.

1955, Jesse was named the director of the new Illinois Youth Commission. This agency set up programs and athletic events for young people who'd been in jail.

Jesse also found that the U.S. government wanted him as a goodwill ambassador. This person's job is to create a good impression of the United States in foreign countries. After World War II, the United States was in a "Cold War" against the Soviet Union. This war wasn't fought between armies. It was a war of words and impressions. U.S. leaders believed that the United States' economic and political system would win out over the Soviet system. U.S. leaders wanted to be sure that the United States was well thought of across the globe.

THE 1956 OLYMPICS

As part of the Cold War, the U.S. government
asked Jesse to go on a goodwill tour of Asia in
1955. He traveled to India, the Philippines, and
Malaya to give talks and to lead running clinics. He
talked about the economic and political freedoms of
his home country. In 1956, he attended the
Summer Olympic Games in Melbourne, Australia.
He was the personal representative of U.S.
president Dwight D. Eisenhower.

In Melbourne, everyone greeted Jesse Owens
warmly. He also saw athletes running as fast or
faster than he had ever run. By the late 1950s,
track athletes were training longer. They had the
support of larger coaching staffs. The athletes ran
on dry, smooth surfaces and used starting blocks.
That year's U.S. Olympic track team won most of
the running and relay events. Members of the
team also took home gold medals in the shot put,
the discus throw, the pole vault, the hammer
throw, the high jump, and the decathlon. In each
of these events, the gold medalists set new
Olympic records.

The star U.S. sprinter that year was Bobby
Morrow. He had come closer than anyone else to

breaking Jesse's record in the 100-yard dash. Jesse was stunned to discover how much he cared about owning the record. "My 100-yard dash mark seemed connected to all kinds of other things—I didn't know what exactly—and if this boy wiped [it] from the books, he'd wipe them all away somehow."

Jesse was watching the Games from the broadcasters' booth. Morrow took gold medals in both the 100-meter and 200-meter sprints. He was the first athlete to do this since Jesse had done it twenty years earlier. Morrow's time in the 200-meter dash was 20.6 seconds. This record was one-tenth of a second faster than Jesse's Berlin record of 20.7 seconds. Morrow also was on the team that won the 400-meter relay race. Its time was a world-record 39.5 seconds. This was three-tenths of a second faster than the 1936 squad had achieved.

No Longer the Fastest

After the Games, Jesse went home to Chicago. He was thrilled at the victory of the U.S. track squad, but he was very disappointed that he was no longer the world's fastest human. Only one of his Olympic records—26 feet 5¼ inches in the broad jump—remained. Owens still held the world record of 26 feet 8¾ inches. Both of these records stood until the summer of 1960, when U.S. athletes were trying to get on the U.S. team. Ralph Boston jumped an official mark of 26 feet 11¾ inches. The 1960 Summer Olympic Games were held in Rome, Italy. Boston also set a new Olympic record with a broad jump of 26 feet 7¾ inches. Jesse's twenty-year-old world and Olympic records had fallen. But he was still a hero in Chicago. He was in great demand as a speaker, and he held many different business positions. These jobs gave him many chances for travel and public speaking. In 1960, he joined Richard M. Nixon's Republican presidential

Jesse supported Republican Richard Nixon in the 1960 presidential election.

campaign. Nixon was running against Democrat John F. Kennedy. Kennedy very narrowly won that fall's election.

The community that admired, praised, and rewarded Jesse Owens also held him up as a role model. He had to set a good example wherever he went. Every day, crowds of people carefully watched and listened to him. Jesse thrived on all the attention, but he also found it a burden. "There are many times now when I don't feel like doing something—signing autographs or speaking for an audience or having dinner with people I have never seen—but the public is not interested in explanations. You got to smile. You must . . . If you are ordinary then the public can no longer look up to you."

MORE MONEY WORRIES

Jesse found out the harsh truth of this statement in the 1960s. He was in his fifties and living well. But then current events and personal problems began to catch up with him. He soon looked all too human to the public.

Jesse had always been careless with money. He had quickly earned a high income in the years after the 1936 Olympics. But he had spent it just as quickly. He had been a failure as a businessman. Several times he found that people he trusted had taken advantage of him.

In the mid-1960s, Jesse Owens found himself in trouble with the IRS again. Investigators discovered that Jesse had not filed any tax returns for several years in the late 1950s and early 1960s. In November 1965, he went to court and told the judge that he'd been too busy traveling, meeting, and speaking to file his tax returns. The court found him guilty of failing to pay nearly $70,000 in taxes. Some people go to jail for this crime. But Jesse was a model citizen, so the judge chose not to make Jesse serve time in prison.

But once again, Jesse faced a money crisis. He owed more than one hundred thousand dollars to the government and to the lawyers who had defended him in the case. Somehow, he would have to make up the debt.

For Jesse, it was almost like starting over again. This time, however, he found that being a role model and a good example backfired. The same public that found him a great role model felt let down. Politicians stopped calling, and charity groups no longer wanted his services. His public relations business failed. "But I still had my friends," he later wrote. "I had them for about four hours after the first story hit the Chicago papers." As a famous man in his fifties, he might have hoped he could slow down and enjoy his success. Instead, he was entering one of the most troubled times of his life.

CHAPTER 9
CHANGING TIMES

JESSE OWENS found himself involved in bitter public conflicts in the 1960s. Other public leaders were facing the same conflicts. One of the issues was the Vietnam War (1954–1975). Beginning in the mid-1960s, the United States had entered a war in the Asian nation of Vietnam. In Chicago, Jesse saw antiwar protesters battle police in the streets. They were making a point during the 1968 Democratic National Convention in Chicago. He also witnessed protests staged by the Black Panthers. The Panthers were fighting racial unfairness in the United States.

(Above) Chicago police face off with antiwar protesters at the Democratic National Convention in 1968.

Jesse strongly disagreed with the tactics used by these protest movements. He didn't necessarily oppose their ideas. But they were militants, meaning they used violent tactics to reach their goals. He saw himself–first and always–as a citizen of the United States. After that, he saw himself as an African American. He strongly believed in the American dream. He believed that each person had a chance to succeed. The person needed to work hard and have patience. Jesse believed that anyone–regardless of race or income–could succeed. He didn't believe in protest marches.

Many young people were opposing the Vietnam War. A draft was in place to send young men into the U.S. military, whether they wanted to go or not. Some young men fled to Canada, where the U.S. government had no power. They chose to do this rather than become part of a military fight they didn't believe in. Jesse hadn't served in World War II. But he didn't believe young men should avoid the draft or flee to Canada.

MEXICO CITY OLYMPICS

The year 1968 wasn't only a year to elect a president, it was also an Olympic year. The

Games were being held in Mexico City, Mexico. Black athletes were joining a growing movement to boycott the Games. The boycott, they believed, would serve to protest racism in the United States and the Vietnam War. Just like in 1936, the Olympic Games became a focus for political issues. Jesse spoke against the Olympic boycott movement.

A few weeks before the Mexico City Games began, the IOC decided to ban the South African team from competing. (It had also banned the country's team in 1964.) The reason was the country's racist policies, called apartheid. To protest against apartheid in South Africa, other African nations had planned to boycott the Games. When the IOC banned the South African team, these African

IT'S A FACT!

The Olympic boycott of 1968 would also focus on the nation of South Africa. At the time, South Africans lived under a system of racist laws called apartheid. The laws separated black Africans from white Africans. As a boycott of apartheid, many African nations were choosing not to send their teams to the 1968 Olympics.

nations changed their minds. They decided to send their teams. The United States would also attend. Jesse Owens went as an official guest of the Mexican government. He worked for the U.S. Olympic Committee as a consultant. He also was a radio commentator.

An astonishing athletic feat took place at the Mexico City Games. It was during the long jump (formerly called the broad jump). Bob Beamon of Long Island, New York, had barely qualified for the finals. But in the finals, Beamon jumped an amazing 29 feet $2\frac{1}{2}$ inches. His jump smashed the world record by nearly 2 feet. Beamon's long jump was the most impressive feat of the U.S. Olympic track team that year. The United States also won gold medals in the pole vault, the decathlon, the shot put, the high jump, two relays, and the 100-, 200-, and 400-meter races.

But African American athletes hadn't forgotten their protests. By tradition, the winners of the bronze, silver, and gold medals stand on a raised platform to receive their medals. The national anthem of the gold medal winner is played. The flag of the athlete's home country is on display.

Medal winners
Tommie Smith
(center) and John
Carlos *(right)*.
They are giving
the Black Power
salute during the
1968 Olympic
awards ceremony.

After receiving their gold and bronze medals
for the 200-meter dash, Tommie Smith and John
Carlos bowed their heads as the U.S. national
anthem was played. But they also raised black-
gloved fists toward the sky. Their gesture—called the
Black Power salute—protested racism.

The protest caused a lot of comment throughout
the world. The IOC wanted to punish Smith and
Carlos. That night, Jesse met with the two sprinters.
He tried to persuade Smith and Carlos to apologize,

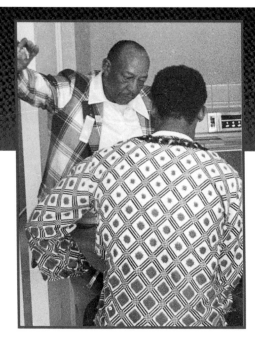

Jesse *(standing)* asked John Carlos to publicly apologize for his Black Power salute.

but the meeting turned angry and bitter. The two sprinters would not apologize. They were forced to leave the team the following day.

WRITING *BLACKTHINK*

The behavior of Smith and Carlos angered Jesse. He thought their behavior went against the American dream of hard work to achieve change. He wanted to speak about his anger and this dream. He decided to begin work on a book about himself. He hired a writer named Paul Neimark as a cowriter. By the spring of 1970, the book was ready. He used memories of his own boyhood and his experiences as an African American athlete. Jesse wrote a lot about his thoughts on race problems in the United States. His book talked about the antiwar protesters and the actions of Tommie Smith and John Carlos. He also talked about militants such as the Black Panthers. Jesse called his book *Blackthink.*

Jesse made it plain in the book that he still believed in the American dream. He claimed that blacks in America were better off than he had been in the 1930s as a college student. If blacks still felt the pain of failure, he believed, they had to look inward for the causes. If they wanted to improve their lives, he insisted, they must simply work harder.

He saved his sharpest words for protesters, militants, and draft dodgers. He believed they could not appreciate the economic chances they had in the United States. He felt these chances were what really mattered. "Sometimes they'll talk with you," he wrote about his militant black opponents. "But in the background is the gun and the knife, the riot and the revolution."

Jesse's message angered many in the African American community. They believed he had lost touch with current problems in the United States. They knew he had once fought racism in Germany. But the 1930s was a different time, and the United States had become a different nation. In his late fifties, Jesse had become a successful, comfortable, and conservative figure. One writer called him "a professional good example." His fame had sheltered him from the racism most African Americans still faced in schools, factories, stores, offices, and on the streets.

A SECOND BOOK

The criticism of *Blackthink* gave Jesse Owens second thoughts. He and Neimark soon began work on another project. It was called *I Have Changed*, published in 1972. In this new book, Jesse was less critical than he had been in *Blackthink.* He used his own experiences as a runner to tell stories that carried an important point. "I'd always been able to get off a fraction of an instant before the other runners," he wrote, " . . . not by listening for the gun as they did, but by watching the gunman's eyes. You can almost

always tell from a man's eyes what he's going to
do next. Too bad it takes most of us a lifetime to
look into our own."

In *I Have Changed*, Jesse wrote in detail about
his struggles. He talked about his own short-
comings as a businessman and as a father. He
acknowledged that blacks in the United States
still faced difficult barriers. He admitted that, in
many ways, his country was deeply troubled. But
he still insisted that men and women of any color
could succeed in a country that offered them
more chances than any other.

At the end of *I Have Changed*, Jesse admitted
that his best days were behind him. He looked
back over his life with honesty. He saw the bad
and the good. He saw the defeats as well as the
victories. Above all, he wanted to keep moving.
"I know I'll drop in my tracks someday," he
wrote. "And I won't really mind if it comes
sooner than it should, as long as I'm making
tracks when I drop."

Jesse's positive message brought him support
from businesses throughout the country. He signed
or renewed contracts with several large corporations.
He traveled widely to deliver speeches on the

themes he had discussed in his books. He was still
in demand as a supporter of Republican political
candidates. He spent much of his time promoting
the U.S. Olympic team. In 1972, Jesse returned to
Germany to witness the first Olympics held there
since 1936. But the 1972 Games, held in the West
German city of Munich, turned tragic. Members of
an anti-Israeli terrorist organization took eleven
Israeli athletes hostage. The terrorists later killed all
the Jewish hostages.

Another event was nearly forgotten in the
shadow of the attack on the Israeli team. This time,

Jesse *(left)* is greeted by officials as he arrives in Germany
for the Munich Olympic Games in 1972.

two 400-meter medalists, Vincent Matthews and
Wayne Collett, turned their backs to the U.S. flag
during the national anthem. Jesse was again called
on to meet with the protesting athletes. They
wouldn't agree to meet with him.

FINAL LAPS

Jesse Owens may have felt as if he was losing touch
with young people and with African American
athletes. But he still was a respected person who
earned warm praise nearly everywhere he went. In
1972, Ohio State University awarded him an honorary
degree as a doctor of athletic arts. Two years later, the
NCAA gave him the Theodore Roosevelt Award for
achievements he made after leaving amateur athletics.
The Track and Field Hall of Fame voted him a
member in the same year. In 1976, President Gerald
Ford presented him with the Presidential Medal of
Freedom. This is the highest honor given by the U.S.
government to someone who isn't in the military.

Jesse still traveled from place to place. He gave
speeches, presented awards, and appeared at
athletic events. His opinions on modern sports and
the Olympic Games still mattered. Fans and
powerful officials listened to him.

He found himself drawn into yet another Olympic problem in 1979. President Jimmy Carter called for the United States to boycott the 1980 Summer Games. They were scheduled to take place in the Soviet capital of Moscow. Carter and others wanted the boycott as a protest of the Soviet invasion of Afghanistan. At first, Jesse supported the boycott. Later, however, he changed his mind. The Olympics, he believed, should always stand above the problems among nations. He announced his support for a plan where athletes would compete as individuals and not as part of a country's team. As it turned out, the boycott took place, and no U.S. athletes competed at the Moscow Games.

By late 1979, Jesse was feeling tired. He was suffering from a terrible cough. For many years, he had been a heavy cigarette smoker. The deadly habit finally caught up with him. He returned to Chicago and checked himself into a hospital. Doctors told him he had lung cancer. After hearing the news, he returned to a home he and Ruth had bought in Scottsdale, Arizona. For several months, he went through anticancer treatments. But the illness was too far along. On March 31, 1980, Jesse Owens passed away in

Tucson, Arizona, at the age of sixty-six. A few days later, his funeral took place in Chicago.

HONORING JESSE

Many different cities and organizations found ways to honor Jesse Owens after his death. Ohio State University built the Jesse Owens Track, a new place for its team to compete, and the Jesse Owens Memorial Plaza. The Jesse Owens Memorial Foundation gave money to young athletes who couldn't afford to go to school. A Jesse Owens Invitational track meet started in New York. In East Berlin, Germany, a street leading to the Olympic Stadium was named after the star of the 1936 Olympics. A stone

This bronze statue stands in the Jesse Owens Memorial Park in Oakville, Alabama.

Jesse Owens's granddaughter, Gina Hemphill, carries the Olympic torch during the 1984 Olympic Games.

monument was also raised in Oakville, Alabama–Jesse's birthplace.

During the opening ceremonies of the 1984 Olympics in Los Angeles, Gina Hemphill carried the Olympic torch. She carried it once around the running track in memory of her grandfather, Jesse Owens. Many thought this gesture by his grandchild may have been the best way to honor Jesse. It was on an Olympic running track, after all, that Jesse had earned his fame. It was on the running track that he had reached one of the high points of his athletic career. And it was for his 10.3-second, 100-meter dash in front of a cruel dictator that Jesse Owens will always be remembered.

IT'S A FACT!

In 1990, President George H. W. Bush presented the Congressional Gold Medal in Jesse's name to Ruth Owens. This medal is given by the U.S. Congress to someone who has achieved a high level of success in a certain area.

GLOSSARY

American dream: a social ideal that pushes for equal opportunity to gain wealth through hard work

anti-Semitism: prejudice and hostility toward Jews

broad jump: later called the long jump, a race in which runners sprint down a runway and leap into the air. The goal is to put as much distance as possible between the takeoff board and the landing.

exhibition game: a public showing of athletic skill

goodwill ambassador: a person who tries to encourage approval and support for the group he or she represents. Jesse Owens tried to encourage approval of the United States and its way of life.

heat: one of several early contests to eliminate, or take away, athletes in a race. Each heat eliminates athletes until the final race is run.

low hurdles: a race in which runners jump over fence-shaped obstacles, called hurdles, that are 36 inches high

minimum grade point average: a level of school testing that meets the lowest standard the school allows

public relations: the business that focuses on encouraging the public to have a positive view of a person, a company, or an institution

racial discrimination: an opinion formed unfairly about an ethnic group. Racial discrimination can lead to racial segregation, or the practice of keeping ethnic groups apart.

relay: a race in which each member of a four-person team runs a section, or leg. The team whose fourth runner finishes first wins the race.

role model: a person whose good behavior is copied by others

sharecropper: a farmer in the southern United States who worked the land for a landowner. The farmer received an agreed-upon share of the value of the crops as payment. The landowner charged rent for the farmer to work the land.

the South: in the United States, the states that fought against the Union (or North) in the Civil War (1861–1865). Jesse's home state of Alabama is part of the South.

starting gun: the loud signal that begins a race

track meet: a competition involving more than one type of running event. Jesse Owens typically competed in several events at a single meet.

Vietnam War: a conflict that took place from 1954 to 1975 in the Southeast Asian nation of Vietnam

SOURCE NOTES

9 William J. Baker. *Jesse Owens: An American Life* (New York: The Free Press, 1986), 11.

11 Jesse Owens and Paul Neimark, *Jesse: The Man Who Outran Hitler* (Plainfield, NJ: Logos International, 1978), 28.

14 Tony Gentry, *Jesse Owens: Champion Athlete* (New York: Chelsea House Publishers, 1990), 28.

14 Jesse Owens and Paul Neimark. *Blackthink: My Life as Black Man and White Man* (New York: Pocket Books, 1971), 125.

15 Owens and Niemark, *Jesse,* 47.

16 Gentry, 55.

30 Bill Libby, *Stars of the Olympics* (New York: Hawthorn Books, Inc., 1975), 67.

32 *Jesse Owens*, The Black Americans of Achievement/Video Collection II. (Wynnewood, PA: Schlessinger Video Productions, 1994).

40 Owens and Neimark, *Jesse,* 61.

42 Ibid., 78.

50 Baker, 93.

55 Gentry, 68.

57–58 Baker, 104.

63 Libby, 68.

70 Gentry, 85.

74 Owens and Neimark, *Blackthink,* 40.

88 Baker, 183.

90 Jesse Owens and Paul Neimark. *I Have Changed* (New York: William Morrow, 1972), 48.

97 Owens and Neimark, *Blackthink,* 90.

98 William O. Johnson, *All That Glitters Is Not Gold* (New York: G. P. Putnam's Sons, 1972), 51.

98–99 Owens and Neimark, *I Have Changed,* 31.

99 Ibid., 152.

SELECTED BIBLIOGRAPHY

Baker, William J. *Jesse Owens: An American Life.* New York: The Free Press, 1986.

Gentry, Tony. *Jesse Owens: Champion Athlete.* New York: Chelsea House Publishers, 1990.

Jesse Owens. The Black Americans of Achievement/Video Collection II. Wynnewood, PA: Schlessinger Video Productions, 1994.

Johnson, William O. *All That Glitters Is Not Gold.* New York: G. P. Putnam's Sons, 1972.

Kieran, John, and Arthur Daley. *The Story of the Olympic Games*. Philadelphia: J. B. Lippincott, 1973.

Libby, Bill. *Stars of the Olympics*. New York: Hawthorn Books, Inc., 1975.

Mandell, Richard D. *The Nazi Olympics*. New York: The Macmillan Company, 1971.

Olympia: Festival of the People. Produced and directed by Leni Riefenstahl. Sandy Hook, CT: Video Yesteryear, 1980.

Owens, Jesse, and Paul Neimark.*Blackthink: My Life as Black Man and White Man*. New York: Pocket Books, 1971.

——. *I Have Changed*. New York: William Morrow, 1972.

——. *Jesse: The Man Who Outran Hitler*. Plainfield, NJ: Logos International, 1978.

Sanford, William R., and Carl R. Green. *Jesse Owens*. New York: Crestwood, 1992.

Speer, Albert. *Inside the Third Reich*. New York: The Macmillan Company, 1982.

FURTHER READING AND WEBSITES

Bachrach, Susan D. *The Nazi Olympics: Berlin 1936*. Boston, MA: Little Brown & Company, 2000.

Goldstein, Margaret J. *World War II: Europe*. Minneapolis: Lerner Publications Company, 2004.

Josephson, Judith Pinkerton. *Jesse Owens: Track & Field Legend*. Springfield, NJ: Enslow Publications, 1997.

Klots, Steve. *Carl Lewis*. Philadelphia: Chelsea House Publishers, 2001.

Kristy, Davida. *Coubertin's Olympics: How the Games Began*. Minneapolis: Lerner Publications Company, 1995.

Krull, Kathleen. *Lives of the Athletes: Thrills, Spills (and What the Neighbors Thought)*. San Diego: Harcourt Brace & Company, 1997.

Nitz, Kristin Woldon. *Play-By-Play Field Events*. Minneapolis: Lerner Publications Company, 2004.

———. *Play-By-Play Track*. Minneapolis: Lerner Publications Company, 2004.

Nuwer, Hank. *The Legend of Jesse Owens*. Danbury, CT: Franklin Watts, Incorporated, 1998.

The Official Jesse Owens Website
<http://www.jesseowens.com/>
Jesse Owens's official site contains a biography, photographs, and more.

Olympics–Fact Monster
<http://www.factmonster.com/ipka/A0114524.html 1936>
General information on the 1936 Olympics including complete medal results.

The Track & Field World of Frank Wykoff
<http://www.frankwykoff.com/>
Information on Frank Wykoff and other famous runners. This site has newspaper clippings from the 1936 Olympics.

United States Olympic Committee
<http://www.olympic-usa.org/>
Up-to-date information on the Olympics as well as its history.

INDEX

PHOTO ACKNOWLEDGMENTS

Photographs are used with the permission of: Library of Congress [LC-USZ62-27663], p. 4; © Getty Images, p. 5; © Bettmann/CORBIS, pp. 7, 23, 29, 44, 52, 55, 61, 67, 72, 77, 78, 87, 91, 95, 100, 104; Jesse Owens Memorial Park Board, pp. 8, 103; National Archives, p. 11; Cleveland Public Library Photograph Collection, pp. 13, 41, 71; The Ohio State University Archives, pp. 16, 22, 27, 33, 35, 54, 59, 65, 82; The Cleveland Press Collection, pp. 17, 19; © Hulton-Duetsch Collection/CORBIS, pp. 47, 62; © Hulton|Archive by Getty Images, p. 50; © UPI, p. 69; AP/Wide World Photos, p. 96;

Cover: © New York Times/Getty Images.